Brett Hardy was born in 1979, in Margaret River, Western Australia. Since the age of 18, Brett has been back and forth from "Margs", having lived in 35 different households between Margaret River, Perth, Sydney and the Gold Coast. He currently resides in Perth.

Brett has achieved many accolades in surfing, including an Australian Open title at age 22. He was diagnosed with Bipolar Disorder Type 1 at age 24.

Brett has zigzagged his way through many career paths, including professional surfer, journalist, bottle shop attendant and now makes a living as a disability support worker. Brett's mental health education includes a bachelor of Psychology at Curtin University (deferred halfway through 3rd year) and a Certificate IV in Mental Health Peer Work at Train Smart College.

Brett has been involved in numerous media roles. He has had many stories published in Australian and International surf magazines and did a six-month stint as associate editor for Australia's Surfing Life magazine on the Gold Coast of Australia in 2003/2004. He has also produced many video works including the surf film *Clown Boots* (2010) and now runs a predominantly surf-based YouTube channel under his own name.

To my DBT counsellor, Jane, for motivating me to write this book.

To Facebook for the 30-day ban that inspired me to finally put pen to paper.

To my partner, Tania, for always being there.

Brett Hardy

BRETT POLAR

AUSTIN MACAULEY PUBLISHERS™

LONDON • CAMBRIDGE • NEW YORK • SHARJAH

A CIP catalogue record for this title is available from the British Library.

ISBN 9781398434202 (Paperback)
ISBN 9781398434226 (ePub e-book)
ISBN 9781398434219 (Audiobook)

www.austinmacauley.com

First Published 2022
Austin Macauley Publishers Ltd®
1 Canada Square
Canary Wharf
London
E14 5AA

Thanks to Austin Macauley for showing interest in my work with detailed feedback, professionalism and enthusiasm. I'm very grateful for the assistance to publish my first book!

Table of Contents

The candid story of one man's progression along a bipolar timeline.

Disclaimer

This book is an opinion piece and not necessarily founded on scientific fact.

Intro

It's interesting that bipolar disorder seems to be characterised as separate to the person, like something they possess. "Oh, he *has* bipolar disorder," to me there is no distinction between the 'disorder' and the person, they are the same entity.

Bipolar Disorder brings with it so many things. Of course, there are the mood extremes that it is famous for, but there are also the characteristic personality traits of creativity, intensity, emotional sensitivity and intelligence.

There have been studies highlighting the correlation between creativity and bipolar disorder aka 'the illness of the stars'.

The other traits (intensity, emotional sensitivity and intelligence) I have studied myself. This research has come from my own lifetime as a bipolar person and being around and observing other bipolar people.

I would say bipolar people are born with these traits. Sure, they can be either stunted or promoted with nurture, however they are with a person for life.

As far as the mood extreme aspect of bipolar goes I would say this is initially brought on when the individual crosses a certain stress threshold.

It's possible that the individual may never actually cross this stress threshold in their lifetime. If so, then the mood extremes would never present. I would say this would be extremely rare.

With each episode, the individual becomes more vulnerable. Future episodes can be triggered by a less amount of stress each time. After multiple episodes a person needs to become wiser and surround them self with care. This could be in the form of meds, health professionals, family and friends or soothing activities/exercises.

With each episode the brain can become more damaged and more vulnerable. One episode too many can result in permanent psychosis. A person may then require permanent care to function in society.

Each bipolar person has different episode triggers. What stresses out one person and causes them to episode may not necessarily do the same in another person.

For me personally, the episode trigger has often been relationship breakdown. I learnt to manage this trigger the hard way. It almost cost me my life, several times.

These days I have a much better handle on it. How you ask? Perhaps we'd better start from the beginning...

Chapter One:
Genetics

Talk to any bipolar person and you can bet your house that someone in their family was bipolar. Statistically, if a parent is bipolar, you have a 10% chance of being bipolar and if you have a twin with bipolar it's 50% chance. I had both.

My twin was diagnosed in 2007, my father was never officially diagnosed but was basically a bipolar pinup boy, had all the traits and mood extremes and sadly without a diagnosis he was never properly treated and is now in jail for life for murder and suffers permanent psychosis.

Unfortunately, this is an all-too-common story for a proportion of bipolar people. I often like to paint the rose-tinted version of bipolar with magical skills and creativity. The harsh reality is that this condition can be extremely dangerous if poorly managed. Not just for the bipolar person themself but for the people around them.

The suicide rate for bipolar people is 10% i.e., one person out of every ten who are diagnosed will take their own life. A scary statistic, and that's just the depressive side of the mood extremes.

The manic side is just as dangerous. If a person enters the psychosis stage, they can do things completely out of character and be a great danger to themselves or others.

Bottom Line: BIPOLAR PEOPLE NEED SUPPORT. Whether they arrange this themselves or via a carer, it is absolutely essential for bipolar people to have support to be able to function in this society.

To expect a bipolar person to just grind nine to five for eternity chasing the CPMK (career/partner/mortgage/kids) unsupported is just lunacy. This is not how bipolar people are naturally designed to operate.

Throw them on a utopian desert island with no deadlines or responsibilities and they'll probably be sweet. They could just roll with the moods and lack of stress and have a sweet old time.

In this western society at least they're going to need medication and as much care as possible to keep the mood extremes at bay.

The nature of the beast is that mood extremes are inevitable. There are life pressures, party temptations and well, 2020.

The key is managing these mood extremes. Basically, you have to be a god damn psychic. When you're doing well you can't take on too many things so that you burn out when your mood comes down. Vice versa when you're down, you can't do too little so that you completely isolate and stay down. Yep, it's a heck of a battle!

I guess it's the price you pay for the bipolar gifts of creativity and intelligence you were granted at birth.

Bipolar people seem to have an extraordinary knack of creating ideas out of thin air. Kurt Cobain, Eminem, Marilyn

Monroe, Carrie Fisher, Jim Carrey, Robin Williams, Amy Winehouse, Andy Irons, Jimi Hendrix ... to name but a few.

These are the ones that have turned their gifts into cash cow \$, but did you also notice that almost half that list is in the 27 club? (Dead at 27.) I think 27 is about that age where everyone has pushed their youthful 'invincibility' as far as possible. Where most discovered the edge and turned back, those in the club did not. In the case of these bipolar celebs, they probably didn't even see the edge. They were too manic to notice.

These celebs may have had plenty of money, just not enough care. So how did I make it past 27? God Only Knows.

Chapter Two: Mood Extremes

Part One (2001)

Ahh! Everyone remembers their first love. For me, it brings back memories of bright summer colours, laughter, giddiness, so fresh albums and of course the youthful naivety that this could never end.

I guess I never really experienced bipolar mood extremes until my first love, at age 21, came to a grinding halt.

I guess for non-bipolar people a first love breakup would result in a miserable couple of weeks. They would feel really down, really lost, feeling like there was nothing that could get you of this pit. For a bipolar depressed person (in this case me) this can go on for six months.

Really really horrible shit. For me, depressive episodes are very internalised and often quite easy to hide. For some people clinical depression means they are unable to get out of bed, unable to move or talk. For me, depression means I can still go to work, fake smile and tell everyone I'm fine.

Meanwhile underneath I'm in agony, ruminating over and over about really negative stuff. In this case the breakup. What went wrong? How could I have changed that? Why can't it go back how it was?

These kinds of tormenting thoughts are a common theme in any depressive episode. The continuous spiralling nature of them seems impossible to escape.

You might get little bits of relief or distraction from certain means, be it healthy ones like exercise or unhealthy ones like substances, but the spiral of thoughts will soon pull you back in.

You will ruminate over and over to a point where it feels like you have no control over it, and eventually your mood starts to spiral down as well.

This is where it gets dangerous. It's impossible to comprehend how you could be feeling this down over a breakup. Your brain's natural defence is to blame everything external; you can't have done this to yourself, it's the ex's fault! It's this person's fault! It's that person's fault!

You begin to act on the anger as if the thoughts are literal. At the peak of my first depressive episode, I wrote in big bold black text on my surfboard, "BODYBOARDING MUST DIE."

I couldn't even tell you what bizarre thinking was going through my head at the time. I do remember feeling very empowered and motivated though because I suddenly had this mission to put an end to the sport of bodyboarding.

Fortunately, I'd always carry with me a keen sense of humour. People didn't take me too seriously when they saw and heard my ramblings. They just kind of laughed it off, but I was dead serious.

This phase in the middle of my depressive episode lasted about a week where I actually had a heap of energy like some kind of hypomanic rapid cycle. (Some bipolar people experience 'rapid cycling' episodes where they can experience both mania and depression within a very short period).

Somewhere along the line the energy came crashing down. I wiped the text off my board with methylated spirits and retreated to the rumination spiral.

After a couple months of this kind of constant ruminations, blaming and trying to figure things out in your head it becomes extremely exhausting. It gets to a point where you just can't take it anymore, and your mind starts fantasising about ending it.

'Suicidal ideation' is a plan a person may have (that they may think about a lot) that involves certain plans to take their own life. For a person that is in a severely depressed state this ideation can actually provide some kind of relief.

The thought that this torment could actually end is a welcoming relief. There does not seem to be any end to the misery. However, your conscious mind pushes on, "They're just thoughts I wouldn't do that," you say to yourself proudly.

Then you add a little something called alcohol. I was probably two or three months into the episode by now and I remember being in a very tense, angry state.

I longed to just be a normal 21-year-old again having fun like all my friends, like I used to before.

I decided to go out drinking with my friends in the pursuit of normalcy. I remember talking a lot about wanting to get in a fight and that I was pissed off with people.

I think I'd been in touch with my ex earlier. I had it in my head that some bodyboarders were going around her house that night so the anxiety that was building was approaching fever pitch.

My friends and I went to the local tavern in Margaret River and American punk rock band 'Strung Out' were playing. I remember being right up the front with a mate of mine and the lead singer was asking the crowd, "Hey you like our accents?" and we started spitting on his face. He was pretty cool about it, just joined in everyone's laughter and wiped the loogeys off his face and started singing.

I had a few bourbons and cokes, which never did seem to agree with me. Mid-mosh, I think my mind suddenly went back to the spiral thinking of what my ex was doing. I started going pretty nuts in the mosh pit, punched some random dude in the head for no reason (which kind of wigged my mate's out 'cause it was pretty out of character for me).

Shortly after, I made a beeline to the toilets. I was slamming doors and pushing past people, swearing at them. The externalising had really kicked in, everyone was my enemy and I was in a jealous rage thinking what my ex might be up to.

Whilst in the toilet, there was only one thing in my mind. I was walking back to my car where my phone was and calling my ex. I kicked the bathroom door of the tavern open, stormed through the crowd bumping into people and spilling their drinks.

I was actually stopped by a bouncer at one point and told to "calm down", to which I replied, "I'm leaving," and began the 500m walk back to the car.

I clearly remember this walk being in such a werewolf-like staunch state, staring down every car that drove past secretly begging for someone to mess with me.

I guess the alcohol (especially once you stop drinking) just multiplies the depression, bringing you even further down than where you were before you started drinking.

I got to the car, snatched the phone, dialled her number and immediately began screaming abuse. "IF THERE'S ANY BOOGIEBOARDERS THERE I'LL FUCKING KILL THEM!!!"

"Who's this?" the ex said. My tone was so atrocious she didn't even recognise my voice. After a more civilised tirade, she then explained she was just chilling at home with a few girlfriends.

I'm not sure at what point it switched, but my dialogue went from abusive threats to pleading for her to take me back.

Of course, she explained this was not going to happen which crushed me to a point of utter despair.

Tears were streaming down my face, and I told her, "I'm going to drive off a fucking cliff!" and I meant it. This was the ideation plan I had been obsessing over for months now.

The next minute or so was a very strange Jekyll and Hyde affair. Half of me was dead set on ending it while the other half was like, "Nah, c'mon man don't do this!"

I was still on the phone with my ex and pleaded with her to stop me from doing it and she told me to think of my family. I really don't remember at what point it happened but something in me snapped. The suicide Hyde side took over, I was doing this shit.

I abused the shit out of my ex, hung up the phone and started the car. Well, I tried to, it wouldn't kick over. I tried again, still not kicking over. Very strange, there had been nothing wrong with my car of late, tried one more time... Nope, not starting.

I slumped over the wheel; anger turned to exhausted tears. I began to feel sick. I opened up the car door and spewed my guts up outside.

My phone began ringing. My ex had called my friend I had hit the town with earlier and he was now calling to see if I was trying to kill myself. I denied everything and said I was just chilling at the car by myself hurling.

I often wonder what would have happened that night if the car had started? Would I have wound up at the bottom of that cliff as planned? Would I have come to my senses halfway there and turned around? Could I really have been another bipolar suicide statistic at 21? Scary stuff.

Such a fateful night. When the boys got back to the car it started in the first go. Wow. Whatever God there is out there I felt closer to him that night.

Mood Extremes – Part Two (2001–2004)

On the drive home, I 'fessed up to the boys that I WAS going to kill myself. The car just wouldn't start. "I hate myself," I said. I was riddled with guilt. How could I do this to my family? To my friends? To my ex?

However, this was the year 2001. I was still three years from a diagnosis and neither me nor my teenage friends knew what the hell to do about it. I was cold, hungover, lost and between us all we thought I just needed to toughen up.

Without any knowledge of a mental illness at that point I thought I was just being weak. I thought I was just hung up on a girl. Looking back, it's obvious it was a lot more than that. I was undiagnosed and untreated.

For a few more months the depression went on. The spiral, the ideation, the guilt and the abuse of my ex. The depressive emotion would build and build to a point that the only relief I could get was by calling or texting my ex with abuse.

This only stopped when her stepdad jumped on the phone one night and told me to stop or it would, "Come back in my face!" I forever thank him for that as it finally put an end to an abusive cycle that I didn't feel I had much control over.

I ended up apologising to her and her parents a few weeks later. It felt noble to do such a thing, but it also made me very sad. They were great people and I had treated them poorly and now I was no longer a part of their family.

Looking back, I could've really done with some counselling. Alas! I endeavoured down the path of denial and eventually discovered something that would help me with relationship breakdown for years to come. BLOCKING.

By blocking/deleting my ex's number I found I could go out, party, even drink and there was no temptation to reach for the phone and abuse. Now the cycle of abuse was broken, my mood actually started to improve. Within a few weeks, in true bipolar fashion, I flipped to the other end of the scale, Hypomania, and had the funnest three months of my life.

I can pinpoint the exact day it happened. It was November 9, 2001, my 22nd birthday. The night started off at my stepdad's house in cute little farming town, Witchcliffe.

I had a great crew of friends around. My twin brother Ryan had his mates there. There were some girls, we were all playing 'circle of death' a notorious card-drinking game that was popular at the time. I remember my mum was a bit annoyed because we were pretty drunk by the time the taxi arrived and some of my mates were underage.

The annual Margaret River agricultural show was on that night (as it often was on my birthday night). It turned out to be a pretty wild night. I remember sculling a stubby of VB in the middle of a cheering crowd next to the tumbler. I then made out publicly with my ex's best friend and subsequently got in a public yelling match with my ex. "You made my life miserable!" I yelled in my true externalising fashion.

We stormed off our separate ways, I ended up making friends with some old enemies and laughing at a mate pissed who had passed out in the gutter at the tavern. Then I went home, slept brilliantly and woke up a new man.

My ex's friend rang me out of the blue. Out of nowhere, I had a new crush on my mind, the spiral was a distant memory and… shit, I felt good again!

After six months of pure hell, "Hards" was back! Laughing, surfing and socialising. Funnily enough, the new crush dumped me a couple of days later via email. It was something about loyalty to her bestie. Actually, my ex sent me a pretty twisted email about it too. She hoped that I was hurting. Probably overdue after my six months' worth of abuse and stalking.

This was really just water off a duck's back at that point. I was high … pomanic. I was sleeping for four hours a night and feeling great. I had energy to burn, I'd taken up skateboarding and made a ton of new mates at the local skate park. I was drawing on surfboards, making video edits, playing tennis and of course surfing.

While at work, in the middle of all this I got a call from West Australian beer company Emu Bitter saying they wanted to sponsor me. You shittin' me? They were offering VIP entry to Perth Cup, Big Day Out and the Margs Pro concert. They were also offering me a bunch of merchandise and a year's supply of beer.

All this just for going surfing like I have done every week since I was nine? I guess I'd paid my dues.

Anyways, the clock ticked over to 2002 and hay was made while the sun shone. I ended up meeting a second love, then moved to Perth to go to university to study journalism.

I collected a bunch of surfing trophies in 2002, including my career high Australian Open Title at Rottnest Island. The ball kept rolling and I eventually moved to the Gold Coast in 2003 to work full time for Australia's Surfing Life Magazine.

I was on the ultimate roll. From 2001 to 2004 nothing could stop me. I had big future plans, a young man with a vision. I felt like bipolar celeb Mike Tyson ranting after a win, "I'm the best ever! There's no one who can stop me! There's no one like me! There's no one that can match me! Praise be to Allah!"

Chapter Three:
Diagnosis

Part One: The Lead Up (2004)

Finally, in early 2004, something started to switch. I became disillusioned with my surfing magazine job. More responsibility was being placed on me and the job turned from a dream gig to an overwhelming burden.

I think my biggest issue was trying to organise other people. At age 24, I'd never really had to organise anyone but myself.

The Quiksilver Pro was in town (the year Mick Lowe beat Andy Irons in the final). My boss/editor Jimmy O'Keefe was a hilarious, hard-working man and a brilliant writer. He was in Melbourne on business during the Quiky Pro, so it was up to me to organise photo shoots, write a contest report and keep things running in the office while he was away.

To my naive mind, this meant simply writing down a bunch of ideas and handing them to our photographers to chase up. I would then go sit on the sand at Snapper and watch every second of the event like the true surf fan that I was and write the contest report.

I guess a more traditional surf journo would be rubbing shoulders in the VIP section. Up there meeting and networking with surf industry honchos and pro surfers alike.

Not me. I had no interest in the surf industry politics and shoulder rubbing. I was all about the surfing. I sat myself on the sand fly-on-the-wall style and watched some insane surfing.

The expression session that year was phenomenal. A young Dane Reynolds was out there as well as a few other big names but really everyone was there for the Irons show.

In shitty four-foot Snapper Bruce and Andy went air for air, and they were enormous airs for the time, making everything too. I was blown away how much better they looked than everyone else. Kelly Slater was in the event that year and even his surfing paled in comparison to the Irons show.

I immediately called up our photographers to see if they'd shot the expression session. Nope. Apparently, I hadn't given them any direction or organised for them any jet skis or passes.

Oops, was I meant to do all that? I think watching all that surfing really made me miss competing too. I'd sort of turned my back on competitive surfing after deciding to pursue a journalism career.

Understandably, I copped a bit of a blasting when my boss returned from Melbourne. I was given an A4 page with all the areas written down where I needed to lift my game if I were to head towards becoming an editor myself one day.

I dwelled on this letter for a couple of days, I think I had a weekend to mull it over. I just felt too young to be taking on this kind of responsibility. For the first time I started thinking about the pay.

The perks of the job were great. You got free travel, lots of free VIP passes and free merchandise. However, the pay itself was basically minimum wage.

I remember thinking, "Shit, I was earning more working on the vineyards back in Margaret River." I think the main decider for me though was the thought of me becoming an editor one day.

I saw how much time and effort Jimmy put into the magazine. The long, long hours, the sacrifices. It was his whole life, he absolutely loved it too and went on to do it for another five years for pretty low pay. He could easy have been making the big bucks writing for a bigwig newspaper like he was making previously in London.

It just wasn't for me at that time, however. I wasn't ready to make all those sacrifices, so I quit. I think Jimmy was a bit shocked, because I'd shown so much excitement and passion in the first few months of working there.

In true Brett polar style, I ran away. Something that would become my trademark. I had every intention of staying on the Gold Coast after quitting the job. My girl at the time was really loving it there.

However, with the C (career) taken out of my CPMK plan (career/partner/mortgage/kids) I started to feel lost.

"What happened to my man with the plan?" I remember her asking. It was strange too because only a couple months earlier things in my life were absolutely perfect.

I had an amazing job, amazing apartment with my amazing girl overlooking amazing surf. Things were dreamy, we would stay up at night watching sex and the city with the sound of the waves coming in over the balcony.

Not anymore though. I had moved into a ghetto pad with a mate in Kirra. The sound of crashing waves had been replaced by crashing neighbourly domestics.

My pursuit of a new job was humbling to say the least. I was getting rejection letters from labourer and dishwashing positions. I started to really miss home.

I set a two-week date that if I couldn't get work, I would think about moving home. I remember getting a call from a group of friends back home that I was really missing. At this stage, the two weeks were just about up, and I hadn't found any work.

My mates were getting ready to go out and were all passing the phone around taking it in turns to have a yarn with me. They all sounded so amped and were having the sickest time. It left me with a huge smile on my face and right there and then I decided, I was moving home.

I broke the news to my girl the next day. Her response was a grumpy look and, "You know I can't go back there right." It was sad but we had definitely grown apart by this point.

I started seeing '2nd love' when she was just 16. We became extremely close and moved into a house together with another friend a year later. This was quite a test for us as we were both so young and had not lived with a partner before.

There were certainly hiccups along the way. The biggest being the night I cheated on her with a uni 'friend' on my going away night before moving to the Gold Coast.

Oddly enough, I had invited my uni friend that night, so she could finally meet the girlfriend I was always talking about at uni.

Well throw a little (a lot of) alcohol in the mix and that plan, along with my self-control, went out the window. The next day I confessed my sins and broke my girl's heart. I think it was seeing her so upset that really showed me how much I cared for her (yes, I know how twisted and ironic this sounds).

I pleaded with her to move to the Gold Coast with me. I had only landed the Gold Coast job a few weeks earlier and at that point wasn't sure if I wanted to go over by myself or with my girlfriend. Living together had kind of fractured our relationship.

In the end, she forgave my filthy cheating ass and decided to move over. She really liked the Gold Coast and we agreed not to live together as it had not worked out too well in Perth.

I moved over to the Goldie first and a month later she followed suit. Things were actually blossoming pretty well for a few months too until I went home for Christmas/New Year's. She decided to stay.

I was having a heap of fun with my home buddies and wasn't keeping in touch with her as much as she would have liked.

I clearly remember her saying some things to me in retaliation like "The Gold Coast would be a great place to be single" and "If you're gonna be like this I want to be single on New Year's."

It was safe to say that the trust was broken... by me, and my cheating. I had pushed her away. Things weren't the same after that Christmas break at home. She was 18 now and becoming more independent and, unlike me, really loving the Gold Coast surf industry. She was working for Brother's Nielsen at the time.

This value clash became most evident the night I got us (and a bunch of friends) tickets to Jack McCoy's *Blue Horizon* movie premiere. I really enjoyed the movie itself but all the namedropping industry and the hob-nobbery around it, I couldn't stand.

As soon as the movie finished, I just wanted to get the hell out of there. She kicked up a stink and said she wanted to stay, I was like, "What for?" and she said, "Meet some people, get a better job!"

This kind of thought stunned me a bit and highlighted what different people we had become. Anyway, I was driving that night, so I dragged her to the casino with my mates and hit the pokies while she stood around understandably pissed off at me.

I guess you can see why she didn't make much of a fuss when I said I was moving home. We still loved each other; we had simply grown apart. She was enjoying her new independent life that she had formed since moving over. ("You go girl!" I can hear all the female readers yelling in unison).

Yeah, I hadn't been a perfect boyfriend, but we still very much cared for each other. We had some wonderful final days together before she dropped me off at the airport.

It was pre-dawn when I started unpacking the boards off of the roof of the car outside the airport. Both our faces were covered in tears. With my surfboard bag in hand, I watched as her little white car drove away. I waved and felt a strange warmth like when you watch a ship sail slowly over the horizon.

Part Two: God Save Me (2004)

Arriving home to Margaret River was a strange mix of emotions. Actually, for a bipolar person it was a pretty volatile mix of emotions.

I could feel the breakup anxiety building. I received a warm welcome from my parents as I moved back into their Witchcliffe home, but I couldn't shake the sadness I felt having just separated from my girl.

I clearly remember rocking up to my mate Mick's house a couple of days later. Mick was a classic redhead grommet who I had spent a lot of time within WA before moving to the Gold Coast. He was five years younger than me, and we shared a similar passion for surfing and hilarious antics.

I remember walking up to his house. There was a kind of depressive sickness now living in my belly. However, this all but disappeared when Mick opened the front door and exclaimed, "Hards!"

Hards was the nickname he'd given me in 1998 and still sticks in surfing circles today. The stoke in his face and gaps in his teeth gave me an instant lift.

I think at the age I was then (24), a sense of belonging in a peer group is of the utmost importance. While the devastation of the breakup was ever-present, so too was the elation of being back home with my mates and family. This devastation/elation was about to prove a dangerous catalyst.

I was loving surfing, there were some grunty waves in Margaret River again. I had a group of close mates and I even picked up a job pretty quickly, delivering linen for a local linen company.

Anyone that knew me and my almost non-existent sense of direction would know that this job would be a challenge. (Keeping in mind this was 2004 and pre-GPS maps).

I was pretty excited to be starting a new life. I was still not dealing well with the breakup though, I was Brett polar, after all. Things kicked off two weeks after I'd been home. My now ex and I had kept in light, amicable contact. This had been a much cleaner breakup than I was used to.

On my yellow Nokia 3210 phone with black keys, I remember calling her from my bedroom in Witchcliffe and asking in casual conversation if she'd been with anyone else yet. She cried and said she'd kissed some dude from her work when she was really drunk at a bar.

I was sober at the time and said that was cool and not to worry about it. I was quite impressed with how well I'd taken it. *Hey, I'm getting better at this breakup thing*, I thought.

However, this one conversation had planted a seed, an anxiety seed, and in the following days it began to grow, fast. The first sign that things were going pear-shaped was during a Margaret River Board riders bus trip to Denmark, four hours south-west of Margaret River.

I was sinking tins (drinking beers) on the way down with everyone else. I think there was a bong getting passed around as well, which combined with the booze is a disastrous combo for me. Things were getting pretty rowdy, and I remember a grommet giving cheek, so I grabbed his hat and threw it out the window of the moving bus. The bus actually had to turn back around so the poor grommet could get his hat back.

Nothing out of the ordinary so far, just kept sinking tins until I eventually passed out on the bus. I remember waking up on the bus at the Ocean Beach caravan park in Denmark. There was no one else on it.

Bastards had left me there. Reminded me of the time my mates left me in a cab outside Mick's house after we got back from the pub. In my stupor, I walked out of the taxi and into the wrong house. I passed out in the random person's pantry and woke up to a broom in the face by the terrified resident's occupant.

Anyhow, I was disoriented on the bus and felt like I'd woken up in some kind of twilight zone apocalypse. Actually, I must have been really fucken out of it 'cause I stumbled off the bus and into the dark, cold, mosquito-ridden toilet block where I decided to pass out again on the tiles.

Freeeezing F'ing cold, I awoke a few hours later to some freaky looking bearded guy asking me if I was okay. He looked like the shovel man off of Home Alone. I think at this point I was sober enough to thank him and then find my way back to the bus. Here I grabbed my tent and pitched it ensuring at least a couple hours of sleep before the contest that day.

The crew got a great laugh out of my story on the bus ride to the comp at Lights Beach. Not me though, I was feeling rotten. There was a joint getting passed around so I had a good toke to see if that would help. Being 24, I was actually still able to surf good in this state. Shit! If I tried to pull this off at 40, I'd end up on a drip.

I got through some heats and then it was out of the water that I started to feel reeeal anxious. For the first time I started to feel a bit paranoid, like something wasn't quite right, something was out of place.

I went for a walk up the beach by myself away from the comp area to try and gather myself. I actually don't remember what exactly I was thinking but I remember feeling a bit delusional. I convinced myself it was just the hangover and went back and surfed the final and won.

I had an epic 6' 2" Dave Lewis board with a green spray on the deck that I absolutely loved. One of those rare magic boards that you wish never got old.

The next sign of trouble was at work. I started making a heap of booboo whilst out delivering and in the workshop. My boss, who was actually an old mate from Primary School, brought me in to the office to see what was going on.

"I think I'm just a dumb cunt," I said, giving him a good laugh. At the time, I honestly thought it was just incompetence but looking back I'd say it was a lot more than that. My sleep hours were starting to reduce.

Then came the energy. Holy shit, it felt like I was suddenly charged by electricity. Kind of like that superhuman feeling you getting walking on a travellator at the airport.

I knocked off work on a Friday arvo. I threw my bag in the Pajero four wheel drive my parents had lent me and charged down to Surfer's Point, techno music blaring. From now on anything playing on the Pajero's stereo was full volume.

The surf was windy and empty, but I went out anyway. Racing thoughts were starting to fly around my head. All of a sudden, a thought hit me, and I got quite emotional. "I'm schizophrenic just like my dad." My dad had been misdiagnosed 'mild schizophrenia' in the '70s.

So, the delusions started. I guess in a strange way it was also insight, noting that something was not right with me. I decided the surf wasn't stimulating enough so I went in.

My mates had pulled up in the carpark. They were asking questions, but I had no interest in conversation. I blurted something at them, blew snot on the ground and they laughed as I headed for the shower. The irritability had started to kick in so when the boys suggested a beer at the local 'Gnara bar' I was like hell fucken' yes!

I got changed, sped to the bar listening to full volume techno then slammed down a beer. The boys noticed something was up with me. I felt like I was ten-foot-tall and had the answers to everything. The boys kept looking at my eyes asking if I was on something. "Nah, I'm just schizophrenic," I said calmly, "it's in my blood mate."

"I think you've had one too many beers," said one mate. The beers did help with the irritability though. "No one else could feel this good without drugs," I thought. Then, it was off to a mate's house for some blunts, (marijuana cigarettes) which sent me into an even more euphoric state.

It was Friday night, and I had the 'Hard's overnight bag' in the car so I asked to crash at a mate's house in town. I was definitely overconfident driving and starting to lose my marbles a bit at this point. As I drove back to his house, I didn't even see a car crossing an intersection, as if it was invisible. It was invisible. Fortunately, we were going slow and there was no collision.

Sleep was basically a thing of the past for me now. Charlie Sheen (a bipolar celebrity who refuses to medicate) once said, "I don't sleep, I WAIT." I must've gone to the toilet five times during the night, my metabolism and anxiety was so high it was now flushing out my bladder.

I took off in the dark and was getting eight-foot barrels on a 6' 10" Dave Lewis design before the sun rose. I was surfing at a place called 'Ellensbrook Bombie' and on the walk back to the carpark I noticed a bodyboard contest on at another break.

"What is this an egg-on-toast convention?" I asked walking toward some poor old mate in my manic state. (Egg on toast was a local colloquialism for a bodyboarder)

"You sound a bit jealous mate," the bloke said.

"Yeah, I wish I could do spinners on my gut," I replied as I walked past blowing snot at his feet.

So, I was back in the Pajero, tunes blaring and driving forty minutes south to a beach break called 'Boranup'. Back on my beloved 6' 2" DaLewy I bolted out the back. On the way out, I saw a mate who had been wasted at a party a couple of weeks earlier. I began yelling at him in quotes that he was ranting at the party, "All chicks are sluts! I don't give a fuck! They can suck my dick!" He was laughing but I think he was pretty weirded out at the same time. He started paddling off like I was a danger of sorts, or was that the paranoia?

I was doing some weird shit during that surf, taking off on closeouts and pulling in bolt upright while staring down people on the beach. Before long, I was back in the Pajero and heading up the coast for another twenty minutes to a break called Grunters.

Again, the surf was pumping. This time I was on my 6' 6" and I think my brain was starting to short circuit. A local bloke by the name of 'Boodji Mick' was out there in his usual hood and way-too-much-zinc attire and I remember yarning to him thinking he had some kind of key to the universe.

I got some sick barrels that session too. On one of them I blatantly ran some dude over in the barrel just not giving a fuck. Okay! Sun's going down now what? I called the boys and I'm not sure if it was me or someone else who called it, but we were off to the nightclubs. The nightclubs were an hour away in a place called 'Bunbury'.

On the trip up, I remember falling into a bit of a down patch. I hadn't eaten anything in days and was rabbiting on about some theory of how every person is an exact 50/50 copy of their parents and that's why I was schizophrenic. The boys were definitely starting to notice I wasn't quite right. When we arrived, I decided to grab one mate and sneak into a packed movie at the cinema next to the clubs.

We sat right up the front and we were pretty fucked up from the bundy rums on the way up. The movie was some real lame romcom and we started laughing really loudly and inappropriately at the soppy romance bits. People up the back started telling us to shut the fuck up, then some hero ran down and started trying to push my mate, who was a younger smaller guy. I shot up in my manic state, "You wanna push someone, push me!" I felt so invincible I wasn't even angry at the guy. I was smiling thinking if the guy touched me, he would burst into flame or something.

Anyways, we just laughed and walked out of the cinema pulling fingers as the crowd cheered our exit. The other lads were waiting outside and one of them had a glass of Bundy and said, "Let's hit the pub!" I grabbed the glass, smashed it on the ground right near another mate and said, "Fuck the pub!" I'm not sure what happened next but yes, we were now in the pub. I was getting my chat on to an attractive blonde. I wouldn't say I was chatting to her in a pickup way but more of a manic all-knowing/absorbing-the-beauty type way kind of like a regular person on MDMA.

Most bipolar people are known to become promiscuous when manic. This is particularly a problem for females as traditionally they are frowned upon for acting this way. For me my manic 'promiscuity' is more a matter of asking a girl a thousand questions and adoring them and wanting them to be in the utopian euphoria with me.

As you could guess, I didn't sleep much that night. I wasn't feeling the best the next day. It was now Sunday and the call had been made to dig out the local river mouth and surf the rapids. I couldn't miss this.

The paranoia, delusions and now grandiosity were taking over. I felt like this day was monumental, perhaps pivotal in human history, that I was Noah here to part the seas and unite the world, and somehow digging the river out was going to achieve this.

After a couple of hours digging with hands and shovels (which helped calm me down a little) a local hippy decided to come down and start literally caving in our hopes and dreams, pushing sand into the trench we had dug. The grandiose plans were shattered and with it went my manic powers. I was more paranoid than ever now and as the boys proceeded to shovel sand onto the hippy's head, I became very anxious and felt the need to distance myself from the conflict.

I grabbed a bodyboard and went out for a few waves enjoying some weird on-my-back riding and whatever else could get my mind off the impending doom on the beach. I came back in and some of the manic energy had returned.

I somehow got talking to another hippy on the beach and we argued about the nuances of opening a river artificially. The delusion in my mind was that as long as he was wearing sunglasses then his words were powerless over mine. I even remember saying, "Your argument means nothing as long as you have your sunglasses on," to which he promptly took them off and touted, "I'm serious," which is when I cowered as though he was Satan himself and I paranoid-ed into submission.

About that time a mate rocked up and started rolling a joint. I asked if I could have a toke and he was like, "Really? I didn't think you were into this stuff."

I snatched the blunt off him and took a big drag. As I watched the river that was now flowing strong, I noticed some rocks starting to poke up and became very paranoid that someone was going to die.

To calm myself down I went back to my car and grabbed a pen and pad where I had begun some writing earlier. In typical manic fashion, I had recently started writing three different books. None of them would end up finished, but I had started an autobiography, a sci-fi novel and a goals book.

I went and sat on the rock with my back opposite to the river rapids and proceeded to write. It must've looked pretty strange to anyone watching. I did this for as long as my manic attention span would let me then walked back to the carpark.

The paranoia set in really bad, I was certain someone was going to die on the rapids, and it was all my fault. Still in my wetsuit I asked some old mate for a lift back to Witchcliffe. It turned out to be the same old hippy mate that defeated me in the sunglasses battle.

Interestingly, we had some really good banter on the twenty-minute drive back to my parents' house in Witchcliffe. This man had no idea I was completely off my rocker.

I saw a neighbour a few hundred metres from my house, so I thanked the old mate and got dropped off next to him.

There I was, in a wetsuit, just casually talking some probably very weird stuff in the middle of the road.

Following casual chats, I wandered off home, feeling okay at this point. My parents weren't home, so I jumped straight in the shower then into some dry clothes and turned the radio on in the lounge.

The announcer asked anyone listening who'd read a really good book recently to call in. The grandiosity kicked back in, and I felt this was another universe-changing moment and I must ring the radio to tell them about my favourite book *The Life of Michael Peterson* that I had read multiple times recently.

I'm not sure whether I messed up the number or forgot to write it down, but that announcer (fortunately) never got my call. I started to feel really paranoid about it.

It wasn't quite dark yet, but I sat next to the phone feeling really really uneasy. I rang my mate's house who I had stayed at the night before to see if anyone could come grab me. My mate nicknamed 'Bobcat' ended up coming to get me, poor guy, as I proceeded to ramble on about how I was schizophrenic, and he was too and that's why our families connected when we were younger and tied in some alien theories. He copped an earful on the car journey, what a legend for rescuing me.

When we got to his house, there were a few guys around and my moods were starting to rapid cycle. I would go from euphoric and all-knowing to paranoid to depressive and always with a high sense of anxiety. The boys took me for a trip into town to try and get me to eat something. I remember crying into a takeaway vegetarian lasagne at a cafe called 'The Green Room'.

My Dad randomly showed up, which I'm sure tied into some delusional theories. I'd had enough by now, I was utterly exhausted, emotional and overwhelmed. I said goodbye to my dad and went back to the boy's house where crippling anxiety kicked into full gear.

I felt the only way to alleviate the anxiety at that point was to watch Kelly Slater sections on surf movies while my mate 'B-rad' stayed by my side. Fortunately, B-rad had a truckload of movies with Slater sections so I stacked up a pile of VHS and DVD's next to the TV and while B-rad slept I watched section after section.

My eyes stared into the TV like the planet depended on it. I don't even know how many nights I'd gone without sleep.

My head started throbbing really badly, and my chest became super tight. I honestly thought I was having a heart attack and it went on like this for what felt like ten minutes. *Am I dying?* I thought. In retrospect I believe this may have been a panic attack.

I was frozen, staring at Kelly Slater in colour. Out of the corner of my eye, I saw two figures enter the room. A strange, strange thing, as I knew no one was actually there. I refused to look directly at the two figures, only looking at them using my peripherals. I could see their outlines and hear them whispering, "Is he awake?" said one.

"Nah he's okay," said another.

Miraculously, I think I did end up getting a little bit of sleep that night. In the morning a little sanity returned. I asked my mates, "Did you guys come and check on me last night?" They said they had not. I had hallucinated, both visually and auditorily.

I said to them, "Fuck, I think I need to go to Graylands." (The well-known psych ward in nearby Perth.)

"Haha, nah you should be okay, Hards," they replied trying to cheer me up. My mate Mick drove me home and I got pretty deep on him, "Things are about to get pretty bad for me I think Mick. I hope you guys can be there for me." In a rare emotional moment Mick said,

"Of course, we will Hards, you're our mate."

I'm not sure if I told my parents (my mum and stepdad) anything when I got back to Witchcliffe. At 24 in 2004, I was living a fairly typical separated life from my parents, keeping my home life and social life miles apart. They soon found out though. There's something about the oncoming of night-time that seems to exacerbate mania.

The paranoia kicked in and I started telling my mum I needed to see the neighbour up the road, then my friends, then my dad, no, my friends! I called my friends and pleaded for them to come around. Three of them came around and I instantly began telling them my theories that my parents had died and were ghosts like in the movie Beetlejuice. When B-rad went to talk to them I was trying to convince my other two friends that B-rad was an alien, "You have to trust me on this!" I kept saying.

When the boys eventually left, I started to become pretty erratic. "Mum the boys are over the road I can hear them calling my name!" I literally could too, I was hearing voices again. By now my parents knew I was sick and my mum became very upset.

I was sure my parents were trying to kill me. When my mum was trying to encourage me to get in the car to take me to emergency, I wasn't having a bar of it. I must've sworn at her at one point because I remember my stepdad saying, "Oi! Don't speak to your mother like that!" which was very rare. My stepdad was a very gentle giant and never told me what to do. This rare display of discipline kind of rattled me and I was just like "Fine, whatever," and jumped in the car, convinced that they were taking me to my final resting place.

As we drove into town, I stared out the window into the blackness of the night. Whatever life I had before, was now a distant memory. Psychosis was now all that I knew, and it wasn't going away anytime soon.

Part Three: Emergency Rooms, Psych Wards and More Psych Wards (2004)

The next four months of 2004 (June, July, August and September) were spent in emergency rooms, hospitals, cop cars, ambulances and psych wards, lots of psych wards. I felt like I was trapped in some kind of public health system pinball machine. Constantly getting belted around from place to place not knowing what the hell was going on.

An initial diagnosis occurred at the aptly named 'Graylands Hospital'. They deemed my episode a 'drug-induced psychosis'. I remember thinking this was a bit odd seeing as I pretty much did the least amount of drugs out of anyone I knew. Why were none of my friends sick? I even asked them when they came to visit me in hospital, "Did you guys get this too?"

In the previous couple of months, I'd probably smoked a handful of joints, dropped a couple of ecstasy tablets and smoked a meth globe once. A psychiatric disorder, as per the DSM (Diagnostic and Statistical Manual of Mental Disorders) cannot be diagnosed until a person has been completely sober for a minimum of two weeks. There was no official mental disorder diagnosis in my family bloodline at that point so the resident Graylands psychiatrist was happy to slap me with the drug-induced psychosis label.

I thanked her for the diagnosis and asked her out to dinner in my still-manic state. She promptly ignored my proposal and sent me home with a bunch of pills. The instructions given were to gradually ween off the meds and SAY NO TO DRUGS!

I followed the instructions perfectly and of course once I started weening off the meds, the underlying manic episode resurfaced, and it was back to delusion-ville. Back in Witchcliffe, I was obsessively listening to my parent's record collection. The Morning of The Earth soundtrack was on repeat as I painted and insisted on calling my mates at four in the morning to go hang at the cemetery. I literally believed I was of religious significance and told everyone I was going to be the next Pope.

To any seasoned bipolar veteran these were very typical signs of mania. However, at this point we had no idea what bipolar was, so it was off to another psych ward to see what was up, this time it was Bentley Hospital.

My mum and I were called into the psychiatrist's office at Bentley where she announced for the first time, I had bipolar disorder. I think I was so doped up on sedatives at the time I remember feeling nothing at all. I always knew there was something different about me, I guess this was just a name for it.

At dinner that night my mum announced it to the family. "Am I?" I asked. I had been so doped up when the psychiatrist told us that I didn't even remember her saying it. Again, I took off home with a bunch of bipolar meds with the hope of finally getting better. Again, they weren't the right meds for me and within a week I could feel the mania coming back. I begged my mum to take me back to hospital. She was quite emotional and didn't want to believe I was sick again. This whole affair had taken its toll on her as well.

The decision was made to book me in to Bunbury hospital, much closer to home than Perth, and for six weeks this time. The aim was to get me settled and on the right medication program once and for all. I was super high by the time I got in there and I was actually sectioned off by myself to keep me from being further stimulated by people in the ward.

When I got a little better, they let another inmate bring me my lunch and hang out with me. I didn't know who this guy was or why he wanted to look after me but him and his big grin were more than welcome. His name was Levi Hone. He told me that when he was first bringing me my lunch, I was so sedated from the injections that I would drool and stare into space while he helped me eat my food.

As I came off the injections, I was still quite manic and remember really excitedly explaining to him and drawing on a blackboard how we were going to be in a band called 'Doesn't Exist' and we would become super rich and famous. He was a great support and would laugh along with me. He would share his own radical stories of being psychotic on ice benders and hitchhiking with people telling them he had to get to the empire state building in New York and meditate.

Once we both got better, we became good friends out of the hospital and hung out a lot in Margaret River. As I eventually got my strength and social skills back, I started surfing lots again. Levi wasn't hugely into surfing and as I gravitated back toward surfing and partying with my original mates Levi and I kind of lost contact.

Only a couple of months later, I was getting my hair cut at home by my mum when we heard the horrible news on the radio that Levi had murdered his mother and five-year-old stepdaughter. It happened at their home in Margaret River, where I had stayed many times.

I was extremely saddened as I had gotten to know the whole family quite well. I was at quite a loss as to how this could have happened. I later heard that Levi had relapsed and gotten back on the weed and meth and become psychotic.

We exchanged a couple of letters and I visited him once in the Franklin ward at Graylands (the criminal ward). It felt good to be there for him after he'd looked after me in my tough time, but he wasn't the same person, that episode had fried him pretty bad and again we drifted apart, this time for good.

Chapter Four:
Recovery (2004/2005)

It took me a long, long time to get back to where I was pre-episode. I would say it was a full year before I felt I was 'back'. The back end of 2004 and front end of 2005 was a slow rebuild. I had to learn how to surf again and eventually got a part time job at nearby 'Prevelly Park General Store' or 'Prev Store' for short.

This job was great. My boss Greg Home was aware of my situation and didn't push me too hard with work duties. It was a very social job which was good for me too. It helped me rebuild the confidence after all the damage I'd done to my reputation during my manic days.

The real reboot for me though was when my good mate Ali, who was as surf mad and adventure-crazy as I was, offered to pay for half my plane ticket to Indonesia. I'd never been to 'Indo', and was just planning to go on a trip up north with my mates that year. Ali insisted I go to Indo with him. He had been through his own mental tribulations at that point and swore it would do wonders for me. I wasn't sure if he was sincere or just needed a wingman but either way I was sold.

I took a month off work, borrowed some money from my parents and come July jumped on a Garuda plane with Ali to Denpasar. It was a trip of a lifetime.

Total culture shock at first. Our first wild night out (straight off the plane) I got completely lost walking home from the Bali nightclubs. I ended up swimming across a bacteria-infested river trying to find my way home. I got my watch and wallet stolen by a hooker as I spewed up in the gutter. I played soccer with some village kids as I walked home with one thong at sunrise. Then I finally found the hotel we were staying in and collapsed into the pool as my mates (who had been a bit worried about me) laughed at my expense.

Feeling pretty ill I only resurfaced from the hotel room once that day to check things out. I got ripped off by one of the alley ladies who lead you down to their shop after wrapping a 'free' friendship band around your wrist. Then they clean your toenails and lead you to an ATM demanding a ridiculous amount of rupiah (equivalent to about $80 Australian).

Humiliated and hungover I returned to our hotel room in a rotten mood. Ali was in and out of the hotel getting his party on. He absolutely loved the place and couldn't believe I wasn't having fun. "Don't worry I've booked us a trip to G-land tomorrow!" he said as he took off out the door again. 'G-land' was the affectionate name for Grajagan in East Java, a jungle paradise known to house some of the best surf in the world. I was so over everything at that stage but thought it might still be worth checking out G-land. Was it ever!

We rolled straight into a week of mind-blowing surf. The first day was average size but very perfect shape. I got the best tube ride I'd had in a long time and came in beaming. Ali's mate 'Burkey' was on the beach when I came in. Burkey was a resident surf guide at G-Land and knew the place back to front. "There's a bigger swell hitting tomorrow," said Burkey as I stood there with my tube-induced grin, "you might even get a proper barrel Brett!" I enjoyed the cynicism but doubted it could get much better than what I'd just experienced. The paddle out the next morning proved otherwise.

Gaping, gaping pits greeted Burkey, Ali, me and another dude from the Sunshine Coast as we paddled out early, no other humans in sight. I was riding a pretty wafer-thin Dave Lewis 7' 0" that felt way too small. Burkey was the man catching big wide bombs on his 7' 6" that were steaming all the way down the reef.

We all exchanged crazy pits for the next couple of hours. I caught one wave in particular that was as wildly ferocious as it was perfect. I raised my hands up while watching this freak of nature ocean corridor twirl and contort all around me. I came flying out and over the back of the wave flopping onto the water in a mind blown state.

This session set the scene for the rest of the week. The swell got smaller, but conditions remained perfect. We all exchanged barrels, bintang beers, ping pong tournaments and laughs mostly centred around drunken Ali pissing in his own bungalong.

When the swell dropped after a week of epicness we legged it back to Bali, full of energy, full of Bintang and full of STOKE. This time I didn't need to be ready for Bali, Bali needed to be ready for me! Hangin' on the 'steps', dancing in da clubs and yelling in the streets, we were on fire. I was unstoppable, I even got laid! Well, it had been fourteen months. My mates were starting to get concerned about me.

I'd lost a lot of confidence since the episode and seemed to be experiencing reduced sex drive from the meds.

I remember saying to my mate's that trip, "I don't really care about sex anymore." Meanwhile they walked around the clubs with their tongues on the floor. So, they were stoked to see me finally get some and I was back baby! The original Hards, party Hards, single creepin' Hards, fun Hards. Damn, it felt good, I had energy to burn, and it wasn't that manic shit. It was pure youthful exuberance that any 24-year-old should feel!

Alas! this had only been the first week of the trip. We then got insane waves at Desert Point in Lombok and more barrels at G-land. On the second trip back though, the waves weren't as good, and I snapped my neck trying to exit a barrel doggy-door style (out the front of the wave).

I'd had plenty of waves by that stage though, so I went in, grabbed a Bintang longneck and happily sipped it on the pondock waiting for my mates to finish their session. With my neck injured, I dedicated the last week of my trip to partying in Kuta. Actually, this was the week I got the one and only tattoo of my life, the Black Swan, on my chest.

The Black Swan is the emblem on the West Australian flag. In this instance it was a symbolic representation of the West Australian people and places that had got me through the 2004 episode. It hurt like fuck and as Ali sat with a Bintang laughing, I sat and stared ahead thinking that the pain was nothing compared to what I had been through the year before.

Chapter Five:
Don't Call It a Comeback! (2005)

I came back from Indo and immediately got a second job to start saving for another Indo trip. I was hired as a kitchenhand at local winery Vasse Felixe. I had also enrolled to study Psychology at Curtin University the next year. A positive to come out of the '04 trauma was my newfound thirst for knowledge. I was determined to study the mind and discover how it could become so corrupted.

I now had a cemented medication regime in Lithium and Epilim each night. I had also sworn a solemn oath to stay off illicit drugs. I felt that there was really no stopping me. My surfing prowess had returned and was even beginning to evolve again.

After five years riding Dave Lewis surfboards, I had switched to local Margaret River shaper Nathan Rose. 'Rosey' and I had grown up together, we shared the same lunch table at school, and we had just spent a lot of that recent Indo trip together. Rosey shared a shaping factory in the Margaret River industrial area with Ding Repair guru John 'Duttsy' Dutton. Duttsy had just started up a clothing brand called Vortex and I became his team rider as well. With this 100% factory blanket sponsorship I went on to win the 2005

Margaret River Classic. The Classic was a historic and coveted event held annually at Surfer's Point. It was a very meaningful win for me.

All the people who had been there for me. My family, friends and old school chums were all on the hill watching the final. It was also a packed audience at the Settler's Tavern for the presentations that night. Neil Thompson was the MC on the night. Neil was the son of my grommet-hood coach Lindsay Thompson (RIP). When it came to the last two men standing on the podium (myself and previous winner Josh Palmateer,) Neil left a giant pause after "and in second place…"

The tavern went dead quiet, pin drop type. Time stopped. "Josh Palmateer!"

I wasn't ready for the eruption. Before I had time to acknowledge what name Neil had called out for second place, the synchronised screaming of the audience lifted me into the air. If not literally then it definitely metaphorically lifted me.

My twin brother Ryan came surging through the crowd and was suddenly front row centre with his arms up high. I held the monster Hamish Mackenzie memorial trophy aloft and we screamed as loud as we could at each other. An incredible moment.

Ryan had been overseas competing on the world bodyboard circuit while I had been sick. He won a contest in Chile whilst I was in hospital and my mum told me that he had won it for me. Strangely tears never came when I finally got to make my acceptance speech. The speech was mostly a dedication to Rosey and Duttsy who'd carried me into this win.

It wasn't until I got back out into the crowd, arms full of prizes, and I was able to hug my mum. That's when the emotion hit. She was the reason I had come this far. She had been at every hospital, every psych appointment, had held me in bed when I was so paranoid, I thought she was going to stab me.

I remembered I was in the middle of a tavern, so I quickly finished hugging my mummy, wiped away the tears and got on it with the boys!

Chapter Six:
I'm Cured! (2006/2007)

A year later I won the Classic again. Things were going so good it just felt like icing on the cake. I'd finished my first year of Psych at Uni, I'd had another epic month in Indo, and I was in love. 'Third love' was a Margaret River girl which meant I was constantly on the move between Perth and Margs. I had study and work in Perth (I had just started at 'Salty Dog' surf shop in Scarborough) and was spending time in Margs with my girl, my boys and my surf. This was also about the time I got bipolar cocky.

I think it was about early 2007, I hadn't really had any psych check-ups for months, hadn't felt like I needed any. Hell, I had not had any sort of mental health issues for about two years now. I was really fit, doing well at uni and work and really happy in my relationship. Why should I keep wasting money on these stupid Lithium and Epilim pills if I don't need them anymore?

I stopped taking them. Cold Turkey. Pretty much everything a psychiatrist would tell you NOT to do. But you know what, I was fine! Actually, didn't notice a difference, and went on absolutely fine. Well fine for a year. "Do you have trouble accepting your illness?" A psychiatrist would ask me many years later.

In case you hadn't already guessed Third Love and I broke up. And almost instantaneously all the bipolar problems returned. My med-free dream run had come to an end. At least I saw it coming this time and this time I checked straight into a private psych ward, Perth Clinic. Here I got the proper care I needed and linked up with a new psychiatrist who I dubbed 'Dr Miracle', who would become my psych for the next five years.

Chapter Seven:
Start Again (2008)

2008 was a very up and down year for me. I was into my third year of psych and obviously (after the episode) my momentum had been stunted. My now ex was overseas on a six-month round world trip, we stayed in touch via email, and you could imagine what that did for my anxiety levels.

Surfing wise things were great. I had only done a week in hospital, so my surfing wasn't crippled like the first episode. In fact, I was still kinda hypomanic when I came out which was awesome for surfing.

I had heaps of energy and was really excited on riding quad-fin surfboards (surfboards with four fins). I did a state title in Geraldton and had a blast. I managed to score a perfect ten in my first heat, did one of my best moves ever in the semi-finals, (a 'Marzo-back' style forehand layback turn named after Asperger's Surfing Sensation Clay Marzo). I only scored a 5 for it, but it is still one of the best turns I've done to this day.

I went on to win the final. A couple of months later I got a fourth at the Rottnest event and lo and behold I had won my first ever state title. Stoked!

In the meantime, my mate Jarrah, (a long-time family friend I grew up with in Margaret River), who was kind of like my relationship counsellor, had convinced me to distance myself from my ex. She was already on the other side of the Earth but basically, he was nagging me to quit with the emails. He told me to stop clinging onto the past and get back on the horse, or maybe he just needed a wingman.

Either way, I took his advice and before long I'd met another girl, 'fifth love'. Funnily enough we had already met at uni, and as fate would have it her boyfriend/ex had also just left her to go overseas. We got along way too easily, and it came at a very welcome time for both of us.

Swept up in the newfound love affair, I was dropping L-bombs after two weeks and the old flame overseas was ancient history. I may have been getting ahead of myself though, as I was still doing some gardening for my ex's mum for some extra cash. I got on really well with her and she helped me through the breakup with her daughter.

Things were going really well with the new girl, so I decided to come clean with my ex and tell her I'd met someone else. No sooner had I emailed her and told her, then I was emailing her again, professing my undying love and crawling back begging her to get back with me.

Obviously, she was confused, my mates were confused, I was confused. It was like that classic scene in Friends where Joey says to Ross, "So if you're going with the new girl, you're doing the smart thing and moving on, but if you go with the old girl. The new girl is free tonight?"

Looking back, it was just the dumbest dumbest decision a person could make. Instead of moving forward and being happy with a truly awesome person I was guaranteeing myself three months of crippling anxiety that would make me lose 20kg. All this on the off chance that it might work out with my ex when she comes back. Who would do this? An idiot in love that's who.

I've often heard and read about people, 'being in love with multiple people at the same time'. After this experience, I'm not buying it. I was definitely confused but I only ever felt 'in love' with one person at any given time. There was no way I could feel that way about two (or more) people at the same time. Well, that's my opinion, anyway.

Okay, where was I, oh that's right, in hell. So, I'd exchanged happiness for misery and coincidentally lost a ton of weight. I was being medicated though so at least I wasn't episoding, or so I thought. I think I was in denial that I was depressed, I kept trying to tell myself, "It's okay you're 'with' her, she'll be home in a few months, and it will all be fine."

There would be a little depression devil on my shoulder that would say, "Nah mate she's overseas partying every night hooking into dudes!"

Fuck it, I thought, *I'll just focus on my surfing.*

The Australian Surfing Titles were being held in Port Macquarie that year. I hadn't competed in Australian Titles since the year I won in 2002. I was actually really pumped on returning to the Nationals. I was keen to check out a place I hadn't been before, Port Macquarie, the bodyboard capital of Australia.

The titles were giving me great focus and distraction from my issues. I won my first heat in some solid surf and thought, "This is great! I wanna win this thing!" I was back in hyper focus mode. I went into the next day of competition pumped, even though the swell had dropped. I bombed.

I surfed like dog shit in typically tricky East Coast mud and my mood quickly slumped to pre-Nationals' level. A few of the crew bought a carton of beers and started ripping in so I thought, *fuck it, might as well have some tins at least I might feel good for a couple of hours.*

We cracked a couple pretty early and by the time we got to the pub for dinner I was proper pissed. I was super skinny by this stage, so it didn't take much. I was doing my blurt-out-offensive-movie-quotes-that-no-one-else-knows thing and picking up people's food off their plates and throwing it at the walls. I was calling everyone by wrong names and basically annoying the shit out of everyone for my own amusement.

As usual, once I stopped drinking the anxiety kicked and I started to think about 'my girl' overseas. I remembered that she had left some kind of number in an email for me to contact her. I stumbled into the caravan park store where we were staying and asked to use their computer. I got into my email, punched the number into my phone and took off towards the nearby jetty in a desperate manner to try and call her.

In my pissed state, I was struggling with the very long number and the keys on my shitty flip phone. I ended up getting through to someone who couldn't even speak English. Frustrated, I simply hung up. I was so pissed, literally and at myself, how had I got into this position again? It was 2001 relived.

All I wanted to do was talk to her, but I couldn't. I didn't even know where she was, or what she was doing. I felt that helpless surge of despair rushing through my veins. The same feeling, I had had in that car that wouldn't start all those years ago.

So much pain I just couldn't bare it. Not this again, I wanted out, I wanted to be unconscious. I remembered I had pills. I went back to my cabin where I was staying. No one else was there so I grabbed my medication container and without even a thought started shovelling every pill that was in there down my throat. I stared at the tear-soaked face in the reflection and just wanted it all to end.

Chapter Eight:
Get Me Outta Here (2008)

I may have just been trying to black myself out, not kill myself, but many people have died this way. For bipolar people accidental overdose can occur just by trying to find balance.

During an episode of mine in 2013, I drank four 500 mL mother cans to get through a seemingly mundane three-hour work shift. I was then so high; I began downing anti-psychotic sedatives on the drive home. When I got home, I had some beers and some more sedatives to try and calm down. In the end though, I had to get my neighbour to take me to the Emergency Ward, not far off a heart attack.

I'm certain this kind of up/down/up/down balance quest has been the cause of many accidental overdoses. I'm thinking Heath Ledger, Andy Irons, Amy Winehouse to name a few.

My saving grace at the incident in Port Macquarie was quantity. I took everything I had in my possession that night which fortunately was only about a week's worth of meds. If it had been a month's worth, I may not have lived to tell the story.

I woke up after the Port Macquarie overdose feeling very groggy. I passed the buck of WA surfer in the Teams event into the much more capable hands of Kalbarri ripper Shaun Howe. I clutched my anxious groggy stomach for the next two days and flew home cold turkey with no meds left to take. That was one really uncomfortable plane ride. As fate would have it, I was seated next to B-rad, the same man who had kept me company during the Slater-viewing paranoia in my first episode. No one in our team had a single clue about my overdose.

Chapter Nine:
This Isn't So Bad (2010)

My girlfriend finally got back from overseas and of course we were on two different wavelengths. I was relieved to have my girlfriend back and my life could start again. She was just trying to figure out where she was, literally, having just woken up in a different country every week for the last six months.

Our first dinner actually went quite well. For the first time she ate more than I did. By now my stomach was the size of a pea. Meanwhile she'd been gorging on all sorts of cuisines overseas and was happy to polish off my leftover nachos.

We got pretty boozy on the red wines and got into some more confronting conversation. I told her more about the love affair I had while she was gone then braced for the retaliation. She said in a real serious face, "I KISSED a LOT of guys," I actually burst out laughing.

"Just kissed?" I asked, "didn't bang anyone?"

"No!" she snapped, disgusted. I found this quite humorous and relieving. I reached back into her nacho bowl shaking my head and laughing. I couldn't believe how well I'd taken it. Little did I know she was saving the best for later.

I gloated later that night, "So stoked you didn't sleep with anyone."

"Wellll," she said, "remember you broke up with me before I went overseas?"

"Yeah," I said nervously.

"I was really upset," she said, "I got drunk that weekend and slept with one of the chefs from work."

I kind of just stared at the ceiling, not responding. Then calmly I said, "That's okay, we weren't together then."

It kind of felt like that Simpsons episode when Mr Burns leaves Homer's name off the birthday card. Homer says to the kids,

"Can you guys go out for a second?"

Then when they leave the room all you hear is "FFFFFFFFF!!"

In all seriousness though, we should've just ended things right then and there and gone our separate ways. That one detail haunted me for the rest of our days. I tried counselling, I talked to my psychiatrist but I could just never shake it. I was mostly pissed off at myself because I was the one who broke up with her which resulted in the hook up.

We didn't break up though, I tried my hardest to make it work, perhaps too hard. Eventually she dumped me after one too many verbally or textually abusive episodes.

So, there I was, drunk, again, walking home from a pub depressed, again. I remember calling her, not in an abusive tone, not begging, just lost, wanting to hear her voice. It was a quick casual chat and a goodbye. I was walking home via the coast from the Ocean Beach Hotel in Cottesloe.

I was looking out at the ocean just south of Cottesloe groyne as I was walking, just thinking of how nice it would be to swim out, way out, and be taken by a shark or hit by an ocean liner, and finally put an end to this pain. Next thing I knew I was down on the sand wearing nothing but my jocks.

I don't remember even being that upset. I was just very apathetic and numb. I swam a long way out too, probably 300m, then... something changed.

I stopped swimming and began wading in the calm water, suddenly noticing how beautiful this moment was. The sound and feel of the ocean around me. The lights back on land and the large rock groyne in the distance. In an instant, the pain had gone. Now I was just very aware of how far out I was in shark-infested waters. It was a long, shark-paranoid swim back in, but wow did it feel good to get back on the beach.

My neatly arranged pile of clothes was waiting for me patiently on the sand, not a soul around. This was a very significant moment in my life. I have faced many more challenges in my life since then. I experienced many more breakups, and my mind has even hinted toward suicidal thoughts since this time.

However, this fateful night where I swam way out to sea in the middle of the night to die, and instead found peace, taught me that suicide is not the answer. It taught me that life is beautiful, that someday my life is going to end, and until it does, I'm going to make the most of every damn second!

Chapter Ten:
Reboot

The one thing that got me out of this breakup chasm was a video project I decided to embark on that went by the name of CLOWN BOOTS. 'CLOOTS' for short was an idea inspired by my old Bali-frother mate Ali. He had recently bought an editing suite and styled a 'Taylor Steele-type' surf movie from archival footage he collected of him and his Mandurah mates.

Stranger than Faction by Garantino Pictures, was an obvious duplication of Taylor Steele's *Stranger than Fiction*. Upon completion, it was premiered at a hall in Mandurah with all the stars of the movie.

Watching all this go down inspired me to make a similar production out of the boxes and boxes of videotapes my brothers and I had compiled between 1990 and 2010. 'Two decades of surfing... two decades of antics' was the slogan for the movie. Over three months I spent every weeknight at my apartment in Mosman Park going through the box of VHS tapes logging the best footage. I then spent every weekend at Ali's parent's place in Pinjarra aka 'the farm' where I would hibernate in the editing suite with Ali and work on the movie.

Just about the time we finished editing for CLOOTS I met 'fifth love'. She was a new love interest from … you guessed it … Margaret River. In true Brett polar rebound style, I was dropping L-bombs within two weeks and broke the lease on my rental to move (again) back to Margaret River ASAP.

I was just so happy to move on from the last devastating breakup that I may have been jumping into things too quickly. When I get into that barnstorming super-motivation zone, ain't nuthin' stoppin' me. Soon enough, I had transferred my bottle shop job to a place called Dunsborough (40 minutes from Margaret River).

I had arranged to temporarily move back into my parent's place in Witchcliffe until I found my own rental. As luck would have it, a couple moved into my place in Mosman Park straight away, so I wasn't out of pocket for breaking the lease. As luck would not have it, Fifth Love and I broke up the night before I was due to move down.

Chapter Eleven:
I Hate You, Don't Leave Me!
(2010–2012)

So here I was, 31 years old, turning my back on a cool apartment and girl-rich city to move back into my parent's basement in a girl-starved country town... single.

I wasn't too bummed though. Since deferring my psych degree earlier in 2010 (due to obvious burnt-out breakup reasons) I'd really turned back into surfing and was more pumped on big wave surfing now than ever before. I had a number of Nathan Rose big wave guns in my possession, including an 8' 8" that I ended up catching the best wave of my life at a place called 'Boat Ramps' in 2011.

So, it didn't all go according to plan, but I loved my new job in Dunsborough. I loved being able to surf good quality waves every day and loved being home in Margaret River surrounded by friends and family.

The CLOWN BOOTS premiere at the local Margaret River culture centre went off, a packed house of about 400 people attended. We even flogged a heap of DVDs at the event. I was really quite amazed that my little passion project had become such a hit.

The biggest surprise, though, was that fourth love was back by my side at the premiere! Margs being Margs, she was already seeing another dude by the time I had moved down. It turned out he wasn't too keen on commitment though, so she came crawling back (not exactly true, I'd say there was more crawling on my behalf).

Everything was set: girl, job, surfboards, pad. I had moved into a sweet townhouse a stone throw from the local watering hole, Settler's Tavern. Fourth love even moved in with me after about six months together. Moving in together would have to be the ultimate test for any couple. This was the second living-in relationship I'd had and just like the first time, it failed.

In retrospect, I probably had moved on from the previous girlfriend too soon. Fourth love and I only lasted living together a month, maybe two. We simply were not well suited enough to last the distance.

So, I was now alone again, in a town with an over-abundance of surf and an under-abundance of available women. In a rap I wrote and posted in 2012 called 'trapped in Margs' I spat about this exact dilemma. I quoted, "The only option for a single brother is a forty-year-old single mother or get on a high school bender and get listed as a sex offender!" Word is born yo.

One thing I was stoked on about 2012 (other than the world NOT ending) was how much better I'd gotten at breakups. The block or no contact or no abuse method worked a treat and for the first time in Brett polar history, I was able to endure a breakup without episoding. I did develop an alcohol habit though.

I had, allegedly, knocked up a local girl after a one-night stand and she claimed that she was going to keep the baby. There was absolutely nothing I could do about it and the next three months were the most stressful months of my life. Alcohol became my way to not think about it. Again, my recurring mate Ali came to the rescue.

Ali had been in AA for a while now and suggested I attend a meeting. I didn't really consider myself an alcoholic, but I did like the idea of enjoying myself without drinking so I went along. I was very inspired by the people there and their stories of enjoying life without alcohol. I decided to quit then and there… Well for nine months anyway. Sobriety was a really cool experience. Those nine months taught me I could be social without being sloshed. I also lost a ton of weight actually and ended up going on more dates than I ever had.

Ironically, I ended up in the psych ward mid-sobriety. Alcohol had been acting as a sedative so once the drinking went, so did my sleep patterns. This episode was about the time my insomnia began. I was officially diagnosed with insomnia about five years later but, it was in 2012 where I discovered that I now needed hefty anti-psychotics to get a good night's sleep.

Insomnia is fairly common in bipolar people. I would say due to the busy mind that comes with the illness. For me I'd say it was also due to the late shift work I did in working in bottle-shops.

At this point, I had forgotten what it felt like to just fall asleep and wake up eight hours later. I could do this as a kid after a day's surfing or school, no problem. Nowadays (if I don't have meds) I could surf for four hours, work for five hours then have a really good meal and still only sleep for an hour naturally. Then it would be ping! Wide awake again with my temperature soaring and thoughts starting to race.

It's something I've had to accept after many years of experimenting with different sleep methods. I've also tested how far I could go with the insomnia. The last time I pushed it, I went two nights without meds (and sleep) before I started hearing voices and hallucinating. Needless to say, I went rushing for the pills to put myself to sleep.

The comedown after taking the pills and sleeping twelve hours was horrible too. I would get sick and be really sluggish for a couple of days. These days I'm happy to take my meds like clockwork and remain stable. Racing thoughts are really not that fun anyway.

In 2013, I got right back into surfing. I had a state title win early in the year and even had hopes of a competitive comeback after making it through the trials of the 2013 Margaret River Pro. However, I was knocked out in the first round of the main event. I had no money and no means of getting back on tour, so it was back on the booze and then back into hospital (due to a no-meds experiment).

When I got out of the psych ward, I found love again ('sixth love'). I was sure this was the one and cancelled plans to star on channel nine reality dating show, *When Love Comes to Town*. I had qualified to be on the show before meeting sixth love. A few months later, sixth love and I broke up. To rub salt in the wounds the tv show came to town right after the breakup.

Not long after that a good mate and neighbour by the name of Chris Boyd was killed in a shark attack. I was devastated. I really didn't have much left in the tank after that.

2014 then started with promise. I transferred my work to a bottle shop that had opened up right next to my house in Margs. This was everything I had been striving for, career-wise, for the last three years.

Then without warning, a letter arrived in my mailbox from the real estate. At this stage I had been in my beloved townhouse rental for three years. The letter said in big red letters, "YOU HAVE FOUR WEEKS TO VACATE THE PREMISES."

I could've sworn they had told me over the phone I was getting another twelve-month lease. Frantically, I called the real estate demanding answers. They had nothing for me except, "The lease was up." I later discovered that the owner had accused me of subletting. This happened after he did a random inspection of the house one weekend when I had mates staying.

It was the final straw. I quit my job at the bottle shop next door, hosted a demolition party at my house that night and trashed the joint. It took me and my parents the remaining four weeks of the lease to fix up the place after that party. Fortunately, I was able to avoid criminal charges. I then packed up my Ford Falcon 'surf wagon', said good riddance to Margaret River and made a beeline straight for the Gold Coast!

Chapter Twelve:
Self Discovery (2014/2015)

In the two years I spent on the Gold Coast, I learnt an absolute shit tonne about myself and my condition. The 10,000 km round trip alone was enough for an entire life of introspective simulation.

I had no job lined up, no accommodation, no contacts, just a destination, and that's exactly how I wanted it. I felt so disenfranchised with my hometown, Margaret River. I wanted to get as far away from the familiar as possible. I always loved the Gold Coast. I'd visited many times and even lived there for six months in my 20's.

Upon my arrival to the Gold Coast, I checked in to the Kirra Tourist Park. I noticed I'd received a Facebook DM (Direct Message) from a bloke called Stevie Lloyd (RIP) who had invited me to a bodyboard movie premiere that night in Coolangatta.

I was pretty sure my brother Ryan was actually in the movie so I called him up to see if he reckoned it would be worth checking out. Of course, he gave it the nod and before long I was in a hotel room with Stevie and a bunch of lads, I'd never met before… and felt completely at home.

One of them, a young bodyboarding-crazy fellow named Dale, was running late. When he arrived, we decided to play a prank and pretend that I was my brother Ryan to see if we could mess with him.

Sure enough, we had him going for about twenty minutes. Eventually, I slipped up and said my DK (drop-knee) stance was goofy, which of course fanboy Dale knew was incorrect and I was busted!

Lots of laughs that night. One of the stars of the movie, Jake Stone, even talked me into busting out a public rap at the premiere again pretending I was my brother. I think about 50% of the crowd bought it while the other 50% were in on the joke and laughed even harder.

I ended up moving in with Stevie a couple days later. It was an insane pad on the beach at Tugun owned by another lad I'd met that night, Liam. One of my lifelong goals had been to live in a beach pad with mates.

The surf out front actually got quite good too. On the right Northeast swell there would be decent uncrowded wedges. Whilst out in the water, you could see Mick Fanning's double storey white palace just down the road.

I kind of slipped into a whole new persona living here. I was a party boy again, like I had been in my early 20's. I was totally pumped on fresh new nightspots, and I was finally comfortable being single.

I'd never really enjoyed being single when I was younger but at 34, five loves deep, I was finally enjoying the chase. There's a reason they call it the 'dirty thirties. At this age, a single man can appeal to all ages. Girls in their twenties, girls in their forties, it truly is a good time to be out there!

I was living a dream life. I'd hooked up a nearby bottle shop job and was surfing some awesome beach breaks. I couldn't believe how comfortable I became in such a short time.

I was very wary of my mental health, too. I began experimenting with drugs again (as you do on the 'Coast') so I established contact with a psychiatrist in Currumbin to make sure I wasn't going to get myself into trouble.

I was very upfront with this new psych about my partying. He was a pretty funny guy, a quiet smiley Chinese fellow who wouldn't nag or judge me. He would just make sure I was taking the meds religiously and send me on my way.

I was on pretty heavy medication that I took nightly. I was on lithium and 300 mg of anti-psychotic slow-release Seroquel, which were basically knockout pills. With this amount of Seroquel, I could pretty much have as big a night as I wanted, as long as I come home and dropped meds to sleep. As long as I had a coffee the next morning, I could even get through a day's work.

The Gold Coast honeymoon period lasted about six months. After that it started to feel like home, and I settled into a more regular lifestyle. Work was steady, Stevie had moved out of Liam's place and back and Liam himself had been staying at his folks Place up at Southport. At that time, Liam was nursing his own mental health issues. He'd survived a psychotic episode a few months earlier. With my experience in the field, I was happy to help him and his family deal with the situation.

So now it was just me, myself and I in this epic bachelor pad on the beach. Ironically though, I had clicked into hermit mode as the work hours stacked up and I no longer had my party crew around 24/7.

Around this time, I dated a single mum in Mermaid Beach. The thought of getting close to a single mum's kids and then having the relationship not work out had always terrified me.

I was surprised how comfortable it felt once I took the plunge and began seeing this woman and meeting her son. It sure was nice hanging out with a genuine person who didn't have a hidden CPMK agenda. She was not sizing me up and pretending to be interested whilst also being secretly interested in about ten other du… oops, I'm ranting aren't I.

I guess you could say by this stage I had developed a certain scepticism for 'pre-Mum's'. In a pretentious place like the Gold Coast where money, power and body image were everything, being genuine stood for very little.

Okay, enough ranting. Single mums were the best I decided. Ironically, this new mantra went dead against the bars I had spat three years earlier in my 'trapped in Margs' rap. "The only option for a single brother is a forty-year-old single mother."

I guess everyone grows up with the ideal image of the perfect partner and situation. You know how it goes… meet a beautiful stranger, fall in love instantly, get married, have aryan babies and live happily ever after.

In reality it may not work out that way. You have to take into consideration divorce, premature deaths, premature births, getting married too young, infertility, all the swept-under-the-rug factors that can spoil the perfect image.

For me, being a 34-year-old bottle shop worker who was five loves deep, I was starting to see through the transparency of that 'perfect image'. I wanted to be with someone genuine. I was not keen on a person who would come running toward me (acting interested) then two weeks later run away when they discover that I don't have the salary or lifestyle to facilitate babies.

I was definitely interested in a single mum who had already done the whole wedding, house and babies thing. Someone who was no longer hiding an agenda and wanted a companion simply for that reason, companionship.

Anyway, the thing with the single mum from Mermaid Beach didn't work out. Then, after almost two years, I considered leaving the Gold Coast. I really didn't want to do so. I absolutely loved my job and the whole coast had become so familiar to me.

Alas, I was no longer comfortable in my living space. Liam and I, besides having become really close mates, were both battling our own mental health issues under the same roof. It was his family home, and I knew it was time for me to go, but go where?

I didn't know that many people on the coast to be honest. Anywhere else I could move would feel like a huge step backward after the Tugun palace.

Then along came old mate Ali, with a room for rent in Scarborough, back in Perth. Perth had always been my backup option if the Gold Coast didn't work out. At this stage, it certainly looked like it was a goer.

I reluctantly gave my two weeks' notice at Nobby Head BWS. It was the most enjoyable bottle-o gig I'd ever had. Next step was planning my going away party. Of course, in the final week of being on the coast I met a girl. It would make me again question my decision to leave.

She had actually been a bottlo customer whom I had regular banter with but never considered that she could be interested in me and my BWS shirt. Well, as it turns out, she wasn't. However, on Halloween Dress-up day at work I wore my Uncle Mick from Wolf Creek costume, and she was mine!

We were quickly smitten, and I was seriously considering staying on the Goldie to pursue a relationship. Then one morning she dropped me off at my mate Ely's house in Mermaid Beach. Ely was a QLD mate whom I'd met with Chris Boyd back in Margaret River. We had done a bit of partying together in the West and he was one of the few people I knew on the entire gold coast.

When my new love interest dropped me off at Ely's house; the next morning he had the pleasure of informing me that he too had recently dated her. This made my decision to leave the Gold Coast much simpler!

Chapter Thirteen:
Perth City Baby! (2015–2017)

I drove for 36 hours straight (with only fuel stops) from Tugun to Ceduna in South Australia. When I got to Ceduna I crashed out in a pretty epic motel by the water. I probably should've stayed two nights; I was absolutely wrecked.

Nonetheless, I jumped back in the surf wagon and took on the Nullarbor. I was still feeling the effects of the Seroquel and had to pull over on two separate occasions to sleep in the car in the daytime.

I stopped for dinner around sunset at a Nullarbor roadhouse. The chicken wings and $14 stubbies of coopers' pale went down like a dream. Feeling better now, I drove a bit further and nestled into a nice little truck stop in the middle of nowhere. I locked my doors and finally had an awesome sleep.

The next morning, I woke up to a silent, majestic desert plain. I hopped out of the car, did a morning stretch and took a minute or two just to soak it all in.

The silence, the space, the beauty. As a human individual I felt then and there that I had arrived. I had run away from my Margaret River past and danced with my demons in the devil's playground. I had got all that out of my system and was now returning home an accomplished man. I was ready to take on whatever lay on the road ahead of me.

I arrived at Ali's house in Scarborough to discover that I was not the only one who had been grappling with mental health issues. Like me Ali had put on a lot of weight.

When I moved to the Gold Coast, I was 92kg, when I left, I was 104kg. I put this down to less surfing, a cushy non-drive thru bottlo job, and of course age. I was now 36.

I guess I hadn't hung out with Ali in person since my final days in Margs, a couple years prior. He would come stay at my house, often when he was unstable. "I'm going to google Hitler," Ali sprung on me one day as he fled out the door, "he's my hero." He later told me he had taken off to the local library, printed out Wikipedia pages about Hitler and went to the local tavern to show people. Ahh, gotta love episodes, Ali was diagnosed with schizoaffective disorder a few years after this. Interestingly, the same diagnosis that my Gold Coast mate Liam would end up with. Schizoaffective is a mood disorder similar to bipolar that also involves episodes. Like schizophrenia it can result in persistent symptoms like delusions, hallucinations and voices.

Understandably, Ali was quite heavily medicated when I moved in with him. He was a far cry from the surf-mad party larrikin who had invited me to Bali ten years prior. However, he was still the same legend bloke, and we still shared the common ground of surf froth, girl froth and gambling froth.

I was still very much in party mode having recently returned from the Gold Coast. I tried my hardest to drag Ali off the couch to come hit the town with me. He was very reluctant to do so. The only time he got excited to go out was if I'd arranged substances (drugs).

I knew this kind of thing wasn't the best for either of us, but I wanted for us to go out and party so badly and have a blast like we used to.

It was during this time that I met my new psychiatrist, who I aptly dubbed 'The Oracle'. He had a freakish way of understanding and predicting my behaviour. He could do this after having only been presented with tiny bits of information about me. I was sure he had access to my thoughts.

I initially consulted with The Oracle at a private psychiatric hospital called Perth Clinic in 2013. This was the episode I had after deciding to go completely off meds. He put me on the stable medication program of Lithium and 300 mg Seroquel (which I was still on three years later when I consulted with him again).

In 2013, he told me straight that if I continued to binge drink and take drugs I would be in and out of psych wards for the rest of my life. I remember I burst into tears (which was embarrassing because he had an attractive understudy with him) and I told him that I didn't want to be the sober guy anymore. I had done nine months of sobriety and I didn't want to go back; it was too hard to keep up when things weren't going well.

I guess he predicted that I would ignore his warnings. He deliberately put me on the really heavy meds of 300 mg slow-release Seroquel. This would pretty much ensure that, if taken nightly, I could party like a demon and still remain stable.

I gave this theory a thorough trial in February 2016 when I had organised to drag Ali along to a Fatboy Slim concert in Perth. Ali, of course, wanted some substances to help him be social and, well, I kind of did, too.

Our neighbour gave us a lift and promised to pick up some substances along the way. It was a little more than we bargained for. I was hoping we were just going to get some MDMA or something. Next thing we knew we were swallowing a shard of meth each. Oh well, it couldn't be that bad after all we'd both tried it in our youth and survived.

About 7 am the next morning we were still flying. We were talking shit at my neighbour's house and showed no signs of coming down. I remembered that I had to surf for Margaret River Board riders in a team's event that morning.

I rang up my team captain to try and weasel out of it. He said that they would have to forfeit if I didn't show. I could feel the racey thoughts starting to come on, so I dropped a couple of 300 mg Seroquel on the drive there to try and slow down. They did nothing.

It was a really hot day, and I was pretty embarrassed to be walking around in my board-shorts with my 104kg girth. I was mostly just hoping that no one would notice my saucepan pupils and inability to stand still.

I went for a couple of swims to fill in time before I had to surf in the event. These swims also helped alleviate the sick feeling starting to appear in my stomach.

Fortunately, the surf at Trigg was one-foot rubbish. Fortunately, again, it was a twin fin event so all I really had to do was go out, stand up on the board and go straight. In the state I was in I would be happy if I could just do that!

I got the job done and got the hell out of there. I dropped a couple more Seroquel on the way home hoping again that it would slow me down. That's now four 300 mg Seroquel tables. A 1200 mg dose would be enough to put most people to sleep for 24 hours. Then I remembered I was rostered on to work that afternoon.

How I thought I was going to go to a Fatboy Slim concert, surf a team's event and then go to work was beyond me. I guess at 26 I may have pulled this off, not 36.

I rang my boss and asked if I could get out of the shift, he said no. I had a couple of hours before the shift started. I wanted to slow down just enough so that I could stand behind a counter without scaring anyone.

I dropped a couple more Seroquel (now up to six times my daily dose). I was trying my hardest to simply relax on the couch before going to work.

Ali suggested drinking a beer, like he was, to help me feel better. I said hell no. I was in agony now. The Seroquel had kicked in by this stage and while my body was completely sedated my mind was still racing. The racing thoughts and Seroquel were fighting each other.

I writhed and groaned on the couch, my heart beating profusely. It felt like my heart was going to jump out of my chest. I started to think of that time I ended up in emergency in Margaret River when I inhaled all the mother cans and beers and Seroquel.

I couldn't be far off a heart attack I thought. I was 36 and overweight, this was no laughing matter. I called up work again and apologised profusely saying I was too unwell to work. To be honest I don't think I would've even been able to stand behind the counter. My legs would've given away.

My boss was surprisingly cool about it, and I told him I owed him one. I hung up the phone and took one last Seroquel, lucky number seven, hoping this would be the one that finally knocked me out. I had no choice but to lie back and watch the struggle of body vs brain.

The racing thoughts were sporadically waking up parts of my body with convulsions. However, with seven Seroquel now in my system the drugs began to win the battle. My heart continued to pound and I was extremely thankful to feel myself gradually sink into a dark peaceful sleep.

It took a week for my body and mind to recover from that incident. I was pretty amazed that I was able to pull that off without a hospital visit. I sure as hell wasn't going to be touching meth shit again! That was the second time I'd tried it. The first time was in 2004 where I smoked it in a globe. It was actually quite mellow that first time, I remember having a good time and then just a throbbing headache the next day.

This second time must've been some new, more powerful shit. It was surely only reserved for the hard-core partygoers. Those who went for days. I definitely like to party but yeah not that much.

I don't think I told the Oracle about this particular incident, but I did tell him that I was going out most weekends binge drinking. He very quickly helped me understand that my need to drink excessively was to fill the void of not having a partner.

This method worked like hypnotism. As soon as he planted this idea in my head things changed. Going out to bars and spending all my money on booze and dealing with hangovers just didn't seem that appealing anymore.

I had discovered a new ailment though, MDMA. This would get Ali off the couch and allow us to have a fun evening once in a while. At my next oracle appointment, I told him that I had cut down the drinking. On the rare occasion I went out now I just took MDMA.

He actually laughed and shook his head. He then went on to explain how dangerous this was for a person in my position. He told me that a person with mental illness, like me, who has had multiple psychotic episodes, and years of drug and alcohol abuse, is potentially just one MDMA cap or one marijuana joint away from permanent psychosis.

Obviously, this freaked me the fuck out. I literally never touched another substance again. The risk now far outweighed the reward. I could still enjoy a tasty beverage or two but the days of risking my permanent sanity for a few hours of drug-fuelled fun or chronic boozing were over.

With my hard-partying days now well and truly behind me, my life began to turn a corner. I started pursuing more personal interests. I was frequently going to the cinema, the library, for walks along the beach and of course my beloved constant, surfing.

In August 2016, I took a trip to Fiji. I met up with a Californian friend called Maddy whom I'd met on the Gold Coast. (Not what you're thinking, this was strictly friendzone). It was a really beautiful trip. We surfed Cloud break and some really fun waves at Namotu. The water was so clear you could view the fluorescent coral underneath you as you surfed over it.

For Maddy's birthday, we went to the most insane party venue I'd ever seen called Beachcomber Island. It was an idyllic desert island that had insanely white sandy beaches. You could walk around the whole island in five minutes.

We had a classic night of dancing in the sand with the other tourists. The locals were super excited the next morning as Fiji were about to win their first Olympic gold medal ever. It was the rugby gold medal that Fiji won at the 2016 Rio Di Janeiro Olympic Games.

Perhaps it was the friendzone companionship I'd shared with Maddy on this trip that sparked in me a genuine longing to share life with someone.

Every evening in Fiji, I would stare up through the palm trees and admire the crystal-clear night sky. You could see every detail of the galaxy and lots of really bright shooting stars. I couldn't shake the feeling of how cool it would be to share these kinds of moments with that special someone.

I was ready. When I got home from Fiji, I began the pursuit. I was no longer going to bars drunk trying to hit on anything that moved. I wanted to find someone I could spend quality time with. I wanted to get to know them, see if we were compatible, and perhaps pursue it further.

I noticed a girl on Facebook who started commenting on my posts. She had a cheeky sense of humour and a cute profile pic and definitely caught my attention. A friend was already trying to swoop on her (actually I think a few friends were). I didn't really make any attempt to engage with her, at first.

I don't think any of my friends got anywhere with her, which ticked a few more boxes for me. On May 1, 2017, I slid into the Facebook DMs (Direct Messages) of one 'Tania Fletcher'. On May 19, I was still in her DMs, in fact we had exchanged DM's non-stop for the last 19 days. We had a very similar energy, a similar sense of humour and obviously felt the same longing to meet someone.

She confessed very early on in the chatting that she was, "40 years old, had four kids, and used to be a stripper." I was very impressed with her honesty (even though she was actually 44).

In 2012, I had pursued a woman who suddenly sprung on me that she had three kids. I took off like the road runner, "Meep! Meep!" Actually, I think dating the Gold Coast single mum had certainly prepared me for this four-kid bombshell Tania had just dropped on me.

On May 19, Tania and I met up for the first time at my apartment. We watched a few seconds of the movie *Bad Moms* and, well, the rest is history.

People often said to me, "When you find the right one everything will be easy." I haven't found that to be true exactly. Tania and I have had huge obstacles to overcome as a couple. I guess the easy part for me was knowing that Tania was the one I had been looking for. She was the one I wanted to share all my experiences with. That part was a no brainer.

Chapter Fourteen: Complicated Grief

Part One (2018)

At age 37, I had finally met the love of my life. However, a girlfriend with four kids was a lot for me to take on. My mental health wasn't the greatest and I had suddenly gone from responsibility-free single creep to role model stepdad.

As soon as I started seeing Tania, I noticed my emotion scale expanded a few notches. I would get on such massive highs after spending time with her. She was the one I had been waiting my whole life to meet. On the flip side I would get massive lows as I attempted to deal with this new responsible position, I had found myself in.

Custody battles, family conflict and relationship hurdles were all coming at me simultaneously. While nothing was going to stop me from seeing the love of my life it was my mental health that again began to suffer.

I had daily thoughts of killing people; who it was, seemed to be irrelevant. As soon as any kind of stress entered my reality, often just regular bottle shop duties, which I thought I enjoyed. Anything slightly strenuous was a catalyst for my brain to delve into the depressive.

I would begin ruminating about a grievance from my past or my present or even make one up in my future. Whoever I was having this grievance within my head I would soon be murdering them horrifically in my thoughts. This would go on for some time until I would eventually crash energetically and hopefully find somewhere to lie down.

I tried to tell my oracle that I was not well enough to do full time hours at the bottle shop. He was always the master of telling me what I needed to hear, not what I wanted to hear. He had a lot of faith in my abilities and would push me to see my potential. "How come you only have to work part-time," he asked, "while the rest of us mere mortals have to work a full week?"

"Well, it's the bipolar, isn't it?" I replied.

"Actually, this is nothing to do with the bipolar," he said, "you are in a job that for you is very mundane and holds no meaningful purpose. Therefore, your mind is wandering."

"What about the homicidal thoughts?" I asked.

"Well, you may have to take a new medicine for that," he said.

"Yeah, no thanks I'm fat enough!" I laughed.

The Oracle had recently switched me from slow-release Seroquel to the quick release version, also known as Quetiapine. This was basically insomnia medication and much gentler on the weight gain. I went from 104kg back down to 95kg in a couple of months.

While I was enjoying fitting into slimmer clothes The Oracle explained that there was now nothing in place to stop my mood going down.

Out of vanity, I refused any extra medication. As a result, the homicidal thoughts and resulting down-moods continued.

91

Eventually, in an act of unconscious self-sabotage, I would get myself fired by live streaming (on Facebook) a bunch of thieves stealing from the store.

This kind of petty theft happened on a weekly basis at the store I was at in Nedlands. After two years of it, I'd had enough and simply snapped. I wanted to show the entire world the injustice that was going on in this store.

Needless to say, my superiors called me in for a meeting a few days later and I was sacked on the spot. I was accused of breaking the code of conduct by placing myself, my staff and my customers at risk. Fair enough too.

I was sad to be leaving a line of work that I had now been doing for ten years. Although, something told me if I really wanted to be there, I probably wouldn't have done what I did.

Little did I know that the sadness I felt over getting fired was about to be monstrously eclipsed. I would go to sleep that night oblivious. Oblivious to the fact that, within 24 hours, an event would drastically change my life, and the structure of my family, forever.

Part Two (2018)

I was quite proud of how I'd taken the sacking. I had taken responsibility for what I'd done and was already pursuing new work. Perhaps a forklift driver? Or night fill? I was going to be getting a nice redundancy from my last job, so I had plenty of time to look.

Tania and her then nine-year-old daughter Harmony were on their way to pick me up from Scarborough for an afternoon adventure. I had just had a typically sizey text from my mum at 3:33 pm. She said she was at her house in Margaret River painting some finishing touches with her husband Dave. They were about to finish up and do the trek back to their house in Augusta because Dave had left his pills down there. There was a lot of nice wording about my unfortunate job loss and to keep my chin up and keep looking for new work. I thought about replying but Tania had just pull up outside my house.

I'll text back later, I thought, and went and jumped in the car with Tania and Harmony. It was a very fun, stock standard afternoon. Tania and I were watching Harmony play on the clip'n'climb at Aloha Surf House in Joondalup.

It must've been about 4:30 pm when my phone started calling. I rarely answer phone calls so when I lifted my phone out of my pocket and saw it was my brother Ryan, I let the phone slide back in the pocket and ring out. It started calling again and as I lifted it out of the pocket and saw it was Ryan again, I knew something was wrong. He never called back-to-back like that. My heart started to race, and I immediately got the feeling something was wrong. I don't know what it was, but I immediately thought something had happened to my dad.

I squashed my own paranoid instinct however and just texted Ryan, "What's up man? I'm at Aloha Surf House with Tania and Harmony."

The phone rang again, this time it was Ryan's wife Leah, and again I ignored it. I told Tania I had to make a call and moved away from the clip'n'climb and called my brother Ryan, heart pounding.

"Are you somewhere you can talk?" Ryan asked.

"Yeah," I said, "what's up?"

"There's been an incident at the Marg's house," Ryan said, "Dad attacked Dave and now him and Mum are in hospital seriously hurt."

"Ah fuck," I remember saying. I looked back at Tania and Harmony playing, oblivious to what I'd just been told.

Ryan relayed more details. He was at the Margaret River hospital where the family had quickly gathered. I looked around in the Surf House, here it was just an average afternoon. The shock was beginning to set in.

Ryan became emotional and handed the phone to older brother Gene. Questions were now firing out of my bewildered brain. "It doesn't look good," said Gene, referring to my stepdad Dave's condition. Dave had suffered a heart attack and was in critical condition.

Tania and Harmony could see something was up. Just the fact that I'd made a phone call was probably alarming enough. When they came over, I said as calmly as I could that an incident had occurred back home, and I had to get out of the Surf House NOW.

It was too much to take in all at once. My mum had messaged me just a couple of hours ago, everything sounded fine, what the hell happened?

I didn't want to get upset in front of Tania and Harmony, so I just blocked it out and talked to my brother Josh on the ride back to Scarborough. It was a relief to get home and feel safe. The shock and disbelief in my brain had started to run rife.

I told Tania and Harmony that I was okay, and they promised to keep in touch as they took off home. I hadn't felt this kind of shock before. I didn't feel safe outside, I didn't feel safe to drive a car, I just wanted to know how my stepdad and my mum were going.

Naturally I didn't sleep much that night, my brothers kept me updated for a while then it was just me in the dark lounge room staring out the window.

In the early hours of the morning, I awoke to see a strange reflection on the tv. It was some kind of light reflection that was shaped like a cross. I had a gut feeling right then that my stepdad had passed away. A few hours later a phone call from my mum in the hospital confirmed this.

I remained in a numb state in the lounge room until Tania came to pick me up to go see my mum. The drive down south to the Bunbury hospital where my mum was taking a couple of surreal hours.

Tania had been through her own family grief with her brother and father passing in recent years. She knew the business quite well and tried her best to distract me and keep me entertained. My mind tried to switch off from her chatter and obsess over details, desperately wanting answers.

Seeing my mum all busted up in a hospital bed brought it all home. I finally let the floodgates open. My mum's sister was there, and I tightly hugged her and my mum. I finally got to let the emotion out that I'd held in for a day or so now.

The injustice of it all was what hurt the most. I'd been staying in that exact house where the incident occurred, just two weeks earlier. I could see that my dad was stressed from living there. He had told me, numerous times, without me asking, that if things got too stressful for him, he would pack his things in his car and leave. Why had he not done that? What had changed? What the hell happened?

I think the bottom line is that EVERYONE, including my dad himself, underestimated his mental illness. No one in their wildest dreams would have predicted that my dad, the gentle wizard, would pull up to the house and run over/park on the garden in the middle of the afternoon.

No one would have predicted that he would get out of his car and walk straight up to my stepdad Dave. Dave had climbed down a ladder where he was painting and asked, "Tone could you please move your car off the garden," to which Tony grabbed a paint roller bar and began beating Dave over the head with it. My mum ran over screaming and tried to break them apart. She was flung onto the driveway breaking her arm, while Dad continued beating Dave with the paint-roller. Dave was left lying on the ground having a heart attack. My Dad then ditched the paint roller and returned to the car announcing, "That should stop the nagging."

No one knew the person who did this. No one saw this coming; no one could have predicted this.

My Dad had become the master of his own condition. He never admitted to any mental health issues, nor was he officially diagnosed with any mental health condition. He certainly knew his areas of vulnerability though. He did everything he could to avoid stressors and remain stable.

Since his marriage breakup in the early 90's, he had steered clear of drugs and alcohol. He never entered another relationship (that we knew of) and maintained a routine schedule to solidify his sanity.

I guess it wasn't until he finally agreed to move into the town rental in 2017 (that his ex and partner had originally built for him to live in) that things started to come unglued.

His surfing days were over by this stage. This was mainly due to a shoulder injury. He had reached pension age, which meant he suddenly had dispensable cash. He was uncharacteristically spending his money on prostitutes in nearby town Busselton.

"They're like doctors!" he was known to say. I think the thing that was most stressful for him though was being back in the position that he thought he had left in the '90's. That was the position of being told what to do.

Once living at the town house, he was constantly coming home to notes telling him what he could and couldn't do at the house. This was obviously getting him riled up, which he was very open about.

As mentioned earlier (two weeks prior to the incident) he lived there with half his belongings still in his car. He was ready to pack up and bail at any moment.

From many reports his mood was escalating in the months leading up to the incident. There were the prostitute visits, an apparent move on a man's wife in town (where the police were involved) and erratic behaviour at a family Christmas party.

The only explanation I can offer is this: The more escalated he became leading up to the incident, the more the insight of "I'm leaving the house if things became too stressful," would disappear.

With the escalation his mind could have become filled with more grandiose and delusional ideas, like his ex and partner wanting him dead (rather than just 'out of the house' as they had threatened on the notes if he didn't comply with the rules).

He was quoted saying many times, "I may have to defend myself." This delusional mania may then have spilled into psychosis, and he literally believed that his ex and partner were trying to kill him. In court, he argued that the nagging notes were evidence of this. He also argued that he killed the man under the pretence that it was 'either him or me'.

My dad is now serving a life sentence on charges of murder and grievous bodily harm.

It is fair to say that I, Brett Hardy, will never underestimate mental illness ever again.

Chapter Fifteen:
I Have Arrived! (2020)

I spent the next two years in support groups, counselling and dialectical behaviour therapy. The Oracle also added Lamotrigine to my medication regime to help prevent the down moods.

In 2020, at forty years of age, I can proudly say that I have arrived. I have finally reached a point in my life where I am stable. I am productive and I have the knowledge and skills to support others.

I completed a Certificate IV in mental health peer work and now make a living as a disability support worker. I thoroughly enjoy this field of work. It is an absolute pleasure being a part of someone else's life narrative. I love being able to support other people with disabilities in their everyday activities and progression on their own personal timelines.

My partner Tania and I run a board riders club in Perth for surfers and bodyboarders. 'Metro Board riders' is a wonderful passion project that we established in 2018. The club is focussed on a sense of belonging and having a good time.

I also co-facilitate mental health support groups for services 'Even Keel' (a bipolar support association) and 'Fremantle Mind'. After being on the participant side of support groups for many years it is an honour to now work on the other side as a facilitator.

After all the trials and tribulations, I have experienced in my lifetime I would say I am most grateful simply for being alive. My experiences have made me wise but also vulnerable. I wrap myself in self-care wherever possible. I tread carefully. Then when I'm feeling good enough, I get out in the world and have a kick arse time!

For the non-bipolar person my life story may seem radical and traumatic. For the bipolar person my story may seem, well, standard. I guess that was the whole purpose of sharing my story. To give non-bipolar people an understanding of the condition. Also, to give bipolar people the strength to know that they are not alone. That if I can get through this so can they. That if they really want to, they can get out in the world and achieve things far beyond their wildest dreams.